Edinburgh Street Rhymes

Doun the close and up the stair,
But an' ben wi' Burke and Hare.
Burke's the butcher, Hare's the thief,
Knox the man that buys the beef.
Old street rhyme.

Edinburgh, Leith
Portobello, Musselburgh
And Dalkeith;

Cockie leekie
Hennie deekie
One, two, three!
Skipping-rope rhyme.

Leerie, Leerie, licht the lamps
Lang legs and crookit shanks.
Play song.

Mary, Queen of Scots
Got her head chopped off—
Just like this!
*Rhyme said while knocking
the tops off wild flowers.*

Isabeller, Isabeller,
Bring aht yer umbreller,
We're goin' away
For a 'oliday
Dahn ter Portobeller.
*Rhyme from a Punch & Judy show.
Punch speaks in Cockney slang.*

I'm the king o' the Castle,
And you're the dirty wee rascal!
Play song.

ISBN 0 550 20355 9

© Illustrations Susie Lacome 1979

© Text W & R Chambers Ltd, 1979

Printed by Morrison & Gibb Ltd.
For W & R Chambers Ltd, 11 Thistle Street,
Edinburgh EH2 1DG.

The poem on the front endpapers is from
'The Poems of Robert Fergusson', edited by
Mathew P McDiarmid. Reproduced by kind
permission of The Scottish Text Society.

EDINBURGH ILLUSTRATED
PAST AND PRESENT

Idea and illustrations by Susie Lacome
Text by Kathleen K Luger

Chambers

Edinburgh Castle

Perched on a rock high above the city, the Castle has defended Edinburgh and Scotland for centuries. The Picts settled there, but were finally forced to flee by King Edwin of Northumbria, who built the first stone fort on the rock. The name Edinburgh may even be a shortened form of 'Edwin's burgh'.

The steep sides of the Castle rock have made it very difficult for the Castle to be invaded. Its dungeons were often filled with prisoners, from Stewart kings to French soldiers. The Castle was not comfortable and made a cold and damp home, as the Scottish nobles frequently complained in their letters.

The Castle has been the scene of many important events. During a dinner attended by the ten year old James II, the young Earl of Douglas and his brother were dragged away from the banquet table and murdered on Castle Hill. This became known as the Black Dinner. During James IV's reign, jousting tournaments were held in the Castle grounds, and were a popular form of entertainment for the townspeople.

Mary, Queen of Scots' only child, James VI, was born in a small room high up in the Castle. Nearby is the room in which the Honours of Scotland are now kept—the Crown, Sceptre and Sword of State.

The crown of King Robert the Bruce (1274-1329), is thought to form the gold base of the Scottish Crown.

Below
Mons Meg, a fifteenth century cannon.

From the fifteenth century until the New Town was begun, the Nor' Loch lay to the north of the Castle Rock, where Princes Street Gardens are today. The Loch was used as a rubbish dump and the bodies of plague victims were thrown into it. Many unfortunate people were put on trial here for witchcraft. The test was simple. They were thrown into the Nor' Loch, if they floated they were found guilty and were later burned at the stake on Castle Hill, if they drowned, they were declared not guilty. It was harsh justice!

During the Edinburgh Festival, the Military Tattoo is held on the Castle Esplanade and a solitary piper plays a lament from high up on the Half-Moon Battery.

Far Left: Edinburgh Castle in the eighteenth century.

The Royal Mile

The Royal Mile, the street which runs from the Castle down to Holyroodhouse, was the main street of the Old Town of Edinburgh. For centuries kings, queens, craftsmen, merchants, churchmen, lawyers and villains have lived and worked there.

The Heart of Midlothian marks the entrance to the Old Town prison.

The Mile was crowded with houses and was dirty, disorderly and smoky. That is one reason Edinburgh was given the name 'Auld Reekie'. Because the street was laid out on the top of a steep ridge and was close by the city walls, the houses had to be built upwards. These tall houses were known as 'lands' and were sometimes as much as fifteen storeys high. Between the high buildings were narrow passageways, known as 'closes' or 'wynds'. One old story tells of a boy who was buried when a land collapsed. His rescuers had almost given him up for dead when he was heard to shout 'Heave awa' chaps, I'm no' dead yet.'

Left: Street pedlars around the Mercat Cross during the eighteenth century.

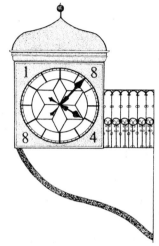

The clock on the Canongate Tolbooth overlooks the Royal Mile. This Tolbooth was once a courthouse and prison and is now a museum.

Different social classes of people often lived in the same building, or tenement, but on different floors. The rich and nobles preferred to live on the floors just far enough away from the street, to avoid the overpowering stench from the rubbish that was dumped there. At ten o'clock each evening the warning cry of 'gardyloo!' was heard. This was the signal for passers-by to watch out, as all slops and waste were about to be thrown into the streets. The expression came from the French 'gardez l'eau', which means 'watch out for the water'.

Castle Hill, the Lawnmarket, the High Street and the Canongate are the four areas of the Royal Mile. In a close in the Lawnmarket—now known as Brodie's Close—lived Deacon Brodie, the leader of a gang of robbers. Looming over the Mile is the steeple of St Giles' and nearby is the Mercat Cross, where hangings and beheadings were carried out, as well as most of the city's business.

Palace of Holyroodhouse

Close by Arthur's Seat are the buildings and ruins of Holyroodhouse and Abbey. The Abbey is mentioned in legends about King David I of Scotland and the Holy Rood, or holy cross. One Sunday, the king ignored his advisers' warnings and went hunting in the dense forest that then surrounded Arthur's Seat. Suddenly a huge stag knocked him from his horse. As the king threw up his hands to protect himself from attack, he caught hold of a cross that appeared on the stag's forehead. The cross broke away in the king's hand and the stag disappeared.

Grateful for his lucky escape, King David founded the abbey of the Holy Rood in 1128. Besides looking after the abbey, the monks were well-known for their beer brewing and to this day breweries still operate in the neighbourhood, as you will smell if you are nearby on brewing days.

The Palace grew from the old guest house of the Abbey. In the early sixteenth century James IV felt that Edinburgh Castle was not comfortable enough for his bride, so he started to build a palace for her at Holyrood. His grand-daughter, Mary, Queen of Scots, lived in part of the tower built by him. There she met her enemy, John Knox, and saw her secretary, Rizzio, murdered.

Many fairy tales and folk tales are told about Arthur's Seat. Among them is the story that King Arthur of Camelot is buried in a cave under the hill. He is said to have thrown his magic sword, Excalibur, into nearby St Margaret's Loch.

'Queen Mary's Bathhouse' near Holyroodhouse, was used as a changing room by troupes of actors giving performances in the Palace grounds.

The ironwork gates at the side entrance to the Palace.

Each year at sunrise on 1st May, many people in Edinburgh climb up Arthur's Seat to wash their faces in the dew. According to legend, this will bring beauty and health in the coming year.

Left: An eighteenth century view of Holyroodhouse with Arthur's Seat in the background.

The Grassmarket

Situated just below the Castle and the Lawnmarket, the Grassmarket takes its name from the corn and grain markets which were held there for several centuries. It was a poor area of boarding houses and inns, tanneries and foundries. As the Old Town became overcrowded, the poor people moved down to the Grassmarket area. An old well, where women used to queue for water, still stands at the foot of the West Bow—the steep street which once led to the Lawnmarket.

Many thieves and murderers were hanged in the Grassmarket. A St Andrew's cross in stone marks the spot where the public gallows stood. One old rhyme describes the path taken by condemned prisoners from the old Tolbooth prison to the gallows.

'Up the Lawnmarket,
Down the West Bow,
Up the lang ladder,
Down the pickle tow'

The 'lang ladder' was the steps up the gallows and the 'pickle tow' was the hangman's noose.

There is an eerie story about a woman called 'Half-hangit Maggie'. Hanged in the Grassmarket in 1728, she gave the driver of her burial cart a fright when she suddenly sat up—slightly dazed, but very much alive!

Left: The Grassmarket in the nineteenth century.

No attempt was made to hang her again and she lived for many years.

In 1736 a smuggler was hanged. Captain John Porteous became angry at the crowd for throwing stones at his soldiers and ordered them to open fire. A few people were killed and some were injured. Porteous was sentenced to be hanged for this action but was later pardoned. This angered the people of Edinburgh and one night a mob broke into the old Tolbooth prison, seized Porteous, dragged him to the Grassmarket and hanged him from a pole.

Right: The public street well at the east end of the Grassmarket.

Below: Once the scene of public executions, the Grassmarket is now an antique shop centre.

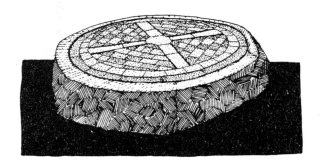

The New Town

A Georgian fanlight window.

By the middle of the eighteenth century, the Old Town of Edinburgh had become greatly overcrowded. The idea of a 'new town' to be built on the flat land north of the Nor' Loch gained interest and a competition was held to select the best plan. James Craig, a young architect, won. His entry set out plans for a large area enclosed within four main streets—Queen Street on the north, Princes Street on the south and St Andrew Square and Charlotte Square at the east and west ends.

Building began in 1767, but people would not move to the New Town until a proper road linking it to the Old Town had been built. The North Bridge was planned as the main road between the Old and New Towns, but part of the bridge collapsed during construction, so that old and new were separated for longer than had been intended. Eventually, the Mound was built in 1781, crossing the marshy Nor' Loch and connecting Princes Street and the Royal Mile.

Left: Early nineteenth century New Town house.

By 1800, many wealthy families were leaving their cramped flats in the Royal Mile and moving into large homes in the New Town. The insides of their new homes were designed with as much care as the outsides.

Georgian architects paid special attention to the fine details of a building — fanlights, door-brasses, ironwork and the plaster and woodwork on fireplaces and ceilings were all carefully designed.

Charlotte Square is a fine example of Georgian architecture in the New Town. The square was designed by Robert Adam, the Scottish architect. Adam's plans were only followed for the north side, as he died in 1792, a year after building of the square was begun.

Alexander Graham Bell, the inventor of the telephone, spent his early life at No. 16 South Charlotte Street. The well-known doctor, Professor Joseph Lister, discoverer of antiseptic, lived at No. 9 Charlotte Square.

The house at No. 7 Charlotte Square is furnished much as it would have been in the early nineteenth century. The large elegant rooms upstairs where the family lived are very different from the dark kitchen and servants' quarters where the maids and cooks lived and worked.

The Dean Village

The Dean Village, formerly called the 'Village of the Water of Leith', lies on the edge of the New Town. At the top of Bell's Brae, the hill which leads down to the village, stands an old building, the Baxters' House of Call. 'Baxter' is an old Scots word for baker and here the bakers from the mills of Dean gathered at the end of the day. Carved on a stone of the building are the words 'In the sweat of thy face shalt thou eat bread.'

Flour milling was the main occupation in the Dean Village. The Water of Leith used to support over seventy mills along its length. Some villagers also worked in the tanneries or wove cloth in their cottages. The cloth was stretched out on the riverbanks to bleach in the sun.

Milling reached a peak in the seventeenth century. Later many mills fell into ruin or were destroyed by fire. As well as turning the mill wheels, the Water of Leith was used as a waste dump. Complaints by New Town tenants about the sewage smells caused by the mills lowering the level of the water, forced the mills to close down.

Reminders of the past are found all over the Village. Bakers' shovels or 'peels' are carved on the granary and bridge, and sheaves of wheat can be found on many walls. Granite millstones stand where one large mill used to work.

The path out of the Dean Village follows the Water of Leith towards the area known as Stockbridge. Overhead is the Dean Bridge, built across the Leith gorge by Thomas Telford in 1832. Beyond the bridge is St Bernard's Well. Mineral waters here were once believed to cure illness. Recently the authorities decided that the waters were probably more of a danger to health than a benefit, and the well was closed.

Above: A carved stone on the 'Baxters' House of Call'.

Below: Old granite millstones with carved ridges for crushing the wheat.

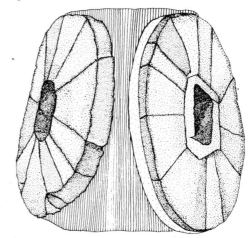

Left: The old bridge of the Dean Village in the eighteenth century.

Calton Hill

Calton Hill, near the east end of Princes Street, was once thought to be a fairy hill. In the seventeenth century people believed that, on certain nights of the year, the Fairy Boy of Leith appeared. He led elves, witches and ghosts to a fairy feast in caverns deep under the Hill. The field known as Greenside was used for witch burnings and the ghosts of these women are said to haunt the area.

In the nineteenth century Edinburgh's reputation as 'Auld Reekie' was fading. The people now liked their city to be known as 'Modern Athens' because of the fashion for copying Greek architecture. The strange collection of buildings on Calton Hill illustrate this style.

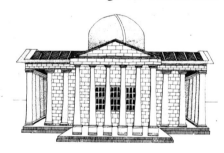

The New Observatory, built in the style of a Greek temple, was used to study the stars.

The City Observatory is the oldest building on the Hill but it was never used. When the building was completed it was discovered that there was no money left for a telescope. Bad luck also hit the plans for a National Monument for the Scots killed in the Napoleonic Wars. It was to be a copy of the Parthenon in Athens, but only twelve columns were built before the money ran out. This 'Greek ruin' is known as 'Edinburgh's Disgrace'.

The ball on the top of the Nelson Monument. Every 21st October the Monument is decorated with flags to commemorate Nelson's victory at the Battle of Trafalgar.

Far Left: Calton Hill in the nineteenth century.

The Nelson Monument looks like an upside-down telescope with a cannonball on the top. Each year, on the anniversary of the Battle of Trafalgar, Nelson's flag signal—'England expects every man this day will do his duty'—is hung on the building. If you watch the top of this monument at 1.00 p.m. each day during the summer, you will see that the ball drops at exactly the same time as the one o'clock gun is fired from the Castle.

On the south side of the Hill is the former Royal High School. Before it moved to Calton Hill, the school was in the Canongate. It was there that a rebellion took place when the pupils were refused a holiday. The boys locked themselves into the school and one of them shot a city baillie, when he ordered the Town Guard to break down the door.

Scott and Stevenson

Edinburgh has always been known for its writers, artists and scientists, especially during the time called the city's 'golden age', which lasted from 1767 to 1832. During these years Robert Burns and Sir Walter Scott were at the height of their careers. Robert Louis Stevenson followed the 'golden age' by a few years.

Left: The Scott Monument at the turn of the century.

Sir Walter Scott, 1771-1832, was born in College Wynd in the Old Town and lived most of his childhood in George Square. He attended both the Royal High School and Edinburgh University and became a lawyer in 1792. Scott preferred writing to law and his poems and novels quickly became very popular.

Edinburgh's 'golden age' for writers was also one for publishers. Archibald Constable, Scott's publisher, was based in Princes Street. Nearby were the offices of Blackwoods Magazine, one of the most famous periodicals of the day, and W & R Chambers' offices were in the High Street, near the Mercat Cross, which is still the company's trademark.

Both Scott and Stevenson set many of their stories in Edinburgh and they made the city's history, people and sights world famous. Scott's 'Heart of Midlothian' from his Waverley novels brings alive the hated Tolbooth prison during the Porteous Riots of 1736. Stevenson is thought to have based 'Dr Jekyll and Mr Hyde' on the double life of the Royal Mile thief, Deacon Brodie. 'Old Leerie', who lit the gas lamps outside Stevenson's Heriot Row home, is known by many as 'The Lamplighter', from 'A Child's Garden of Verses'.

Robert Louis Stevenson, 1850-1894, lived most of his childhood at 17 Heriot Row in the New Town. Due to ill-health, he spent much of his life away from Edinburgh, but more than any other writer, he was influenced by Edinburgh and its unusual characters.

There are several monuments in memory of these men. The best known is the Scott Monument on Princes Street. The 61 metre high spire was finished in 1844 and features sculptures of Scott and characters from his novels. The steep climb up the tower is worth the effort, as on a clear day, one of Edinburgh's best views can be seen from the top.

The Royal Botanic Gardens

In 1670 a small medical or physic garden was laid out in the grounds of Holyroodhouse by two Edinburgh doctors, Andrew Balfour and Robert Sibbald. This was the beginning of today's Royal Botanic Gardens. Seventeenth century medicine used herbs for curing many illnesses and so the physic garden contained useful plants such as chamomile for treating nerve troubles and lily of the valley for loss of memory.

As the number of plants increased, more space was needed and the Gardens moved several times. Finally in 1827 they were moved to their present site at Inverleith. It was no longer a simple herb garden, but now a collection of unusual plants and trees from all over the world.

The Botanics, as the Gardens are usually called, changed under the care of each head keeper. Some of the keepers spent most of their time collecting exotic plants from places such as China, India, the Himalayas and North America. Often these collecting trips could be extremely dangerous. Those keepers who stayed at home concentrated on the layout of the Gardens.

The problem of moving large trees was solved by an invention of the Garden staff. A machine which could transplant a tree weighing up to 1,500 kilograms was built. This machine moved a two

hundred year old tree known as 'Sutherland's yew' to Inverleith. Here the tree became quite a landmark until it was blown down in the terrible gales that struck the south of Scotland in 1968.

In the 1860s a debate broke out over the opening of the Botanics on Sunday afternoons. Opening them would mean that the poorer people of Edinburgh could walk there on their one free day of the week. But some of the wealthier people did not approve. The argument that a visit to the Gardens would improve both health and manners eventually won and the Gardens were kept open.

A modern sculpture by Henry Moore on the lawn of Inverleith House in the Botanics.

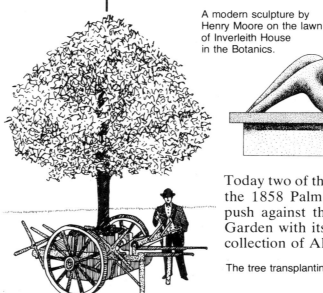

Today two of the most popular areas are the 1858 Palm House where the trees push against the ceiling and the Rock Garden with its twisting paths and fine collection of Alpine plants.

The tree transplanting machine.

Left: The Royal Botanic Gardens in the nineteenth century.

Newhaven Fishwives

'Caller herrin', new drawn frae the Forth.
Wha'll buy my caller herrin'?'

The calls of the Newhaven fishwives were familiar sounds in Edinburgh until about twenty years ago. 'Caller cod' 'caller herrin' and 'caller ou'—fresh cod, herring and oysters—were the cries called by the fishwives as they walked all over the city, selling fish from the baskets, or creels they carried on their backs. They wore gaily coloured shawls and blue and white striped aprons on top of navy-blue skirts, which were looped up to show brightly striped petticoats.

Every morning the fishwives went to Newhaven harbour to buy fish to sell in the city. Usually they bought sole, haddock, whiting, herring and cod and often their creels weighed as much as 50 kilograms. Some of the women had set routes with regular customers, while others simply peddled their fish round the streets. One popular way of cooking herring bought from the fishwives was to rub the fish with salt, then roll in oatmeal and fry in hot fat.

Newhaven was especially well-known for its oysters. The villagers guarded the oyster beds carefully in case anyone tried to raid them. Several fights did break out

A ship's anchor in a Newhaven street.

between boats from Newhaven and boats from other villages along the Forth. From 1850 onwards, oysters became scarce around Newhaven due to overfishing and pollution. Now the oyster beds are empty.

There are very few street pedlars left in Edinburgh. Although the fishmarket is still at Newhaven, fish is delivered throughout the city in vans. Only a few horse-drawn carts still deliver coal, milk or beer to customers. Sometimes French onion sellers, or 'ingin johnnies', arrive in the city on their bicycles and peddle their strings of onions from door to door.

The lighthouse at the entrance to Newhaven harbour.

Left: Fishwives in Newhaven Village at the beginning of the twentieth century.

Round about Edinburgh

Cramond Village, which appears in picture 1, stands at the mouth of the River Almond where it enters the Firth of Forth. The remains of a Roman fort, dating from the second century AD, have been discovered in the old churchyard. Throughout the village many Roman coins, carved stones and bottles have been found and new archaeological digs are now in progress. The River Almond was once busy with supply boats and iron mills, today it is one of Edinburgh's main yachting centres.

Left:

1	3
2	4

1. Cramond Village.
2. Forth Railway Bridge.
3. Craigmillar Castle ruins.
4. Portobello beach.

A Roman soldier on a Cramond Village sign.

The village of Queensferry takes its name from the crossings Queen Margaret made between Edinburgh and Fife in the eleventh century. In 1873 work was begun here on the railway bridge shown in picture 2, under the direction of Sir Thomas Bouche, designer of the Tay Bridge. When the Tay Bridge collapsed in a storm in 1879, Bouche was dismissed and two new designers were hired. The unusual ironwork and large towers of the Railway Bridge contrast with the sparse lines of the modern Forth Road Bridge opened in 1964.

The ruins of Craigmillar Castle, just south of Edinburgh, are shown in picture 3. The royal Stewart family is connected with the Castle's history. In 1479 James III, fearing a revolt, used the Castle as a prison for his brother the Earl of Mar, who eventually died there. The plot by three Scottish nobles to kill Darnley—Mary, Queen of Scots' unpopular husband—is thought to have been planned at Craigmillar.

Picture 4 shows Portobello beach. From the late eighteenth century until recent years, Portobello was Edinburgh's holiday resort. Each June, the wealthy moved to their fancy summer homes at the beach, while most people went there for a day's holiday. The beach was crowded with swimmers, Punch and Judy shows and 'Hokey Pokey men' selling ice cream.

Hokey Pokey penny a lump
That's the stuff to make you jump!

Princes Street

Although a close in the Royal Mile or a crescent in the New Town are more typically Edinburgh, Princes Street is what people remember most about the city. The street was first to be called Saint Giles Street, but George III insisted that it be named for his two sons.

Joining Princes Street to the Old Town is the Mound, a steep curving road leading up to the Royal Mile. It was built on rubble left over from the construction of the New Town. On the Mound are two of Edinburgh's largest art galleries—The Royal Scottish Academy and the National Gallery. Both galleries, as well as Robert Adam's Register House at the east end of Princes Street, are classical in style and remind us of Edinburgh's obsession with being the 'Athens of the North'.

On either side of the Mound are the Princes Street Gardens—laid out on the bed of the old Nor' Loch. Only people who lived within the area of Princes Street were to have keys, which cost a pound. One city locksmith made a fortune selling keys to people who were not supposed to have them.

The statue of the Duke of Wellington outside Register House, the Scottish Public Records Office. Since 1855 all births, deaths and marriages in Scotland have been recorded here.

Left: Princes Street during the Edinburgh Festival.

In the graveyard of St Cuthbert's Church, at the west end of Princes Street, is a small stone tower built in the nineteenth century. From this tower relatives guarded graves against 'resurrectionists', people who robbed graves and sold the bodies to doctors for study.

The Floral Clock in Princes Street Gardens is planted every summer and a cuckoo pops out to signal the quarter hour.

Since 1947, late summer has come to mean the Edinburgh International Festival. Drama, opera, dance, art, music and films are all represented by world-famous artists. Started after the Second World War, the Festival has grown yearly and thousands of visitors crowd into Edinburgh to attend performances. Every morning, the Street becomes the focal point of the city with a parade of Pipe Bands.

Famous People of Edinburgh

John Knox 1513-1572

John Knox was a religious reformer who played an important part in changing the religion of Scotland from Catholic to Protestant. After the French defeated Knox and a group of Protestants at St Andrews' Castle, he was taken prisoner and spent eighteen months as a slave on a French galley ship. When he was released Knox returned to Scotland where he became a strong opponent of Mary, Queen of Scots. Knox was well-known for his forceful preaching in St Giles' but it is doubtful whether he ever lived in the building called John Knox's House.

Mary, Queen of Scots 1542-1587

Mary became Queen when she was only a few days old and spent her childhood in France. She returned to Scotland in 1561 but found the life very different from that of France.

Mary's Catholic religion made her unpopular with the country's growing number of Protestants. After her third marriage to the suspected murderer Bothwell, Mary lost the support of her nobles and was forced to give up her crown and leave the country. For eighteen years she lived in England as a prisoner until she was beheaded in 1587 for supposedly plotting against Elizabeth I.

Deacon Brodie died 1788

Brodie was a member of the town council, a Deacon of the Cabinetmakers Guild and was one of Edinburgh's cleverest criminals. During the day he would often work as a cabinetmaker in many of the city's wealthy homes. Then at night, he would return to those same houses to rob them.

He was identified when one of his partners gave evidence to get the reward that was offered by the authorities. Brodie escaped from Edinburgh but was recognised while on a boat to Holland. He was traced and brought back for trial, then hanged.